Kennel Cough

Kennel Cough in Pets: Facts and Information

Including Bordetella, Canine Parainfluenza, vaccine, symptoms, diagnosing, duration, treatment, relief, and much more.

By: Lolly Brown

Foreword

Most dog owners are aware of something called "kennel cough" because they take their pet to "doggy day care" or to a boarding facility. No kennel cough vaccination? No admission. Why? Because kennel cough is a highly contagious respiratory disease. All an infected dog has to do is breathe around other dogs and transmission is all but certain.

Even in closed environments that are large, well ventilated, and clean, kennel cough can spread. One infected dog can easily cause a major outbreak, which is why the problem is so prevalent in animal shelters where, sadly, it can be a death sentence.

Infected animals are routinely put on the "too sick to adopt" list and euthanized because the facilities, chronically strapped for funds, can't afford to house and treat the dogs until the disease resolves.

The infectious agents responsible for kennel cough live in the animal's airways and become airborne as microscopic water or dust particles. The illness can be caused by a single bacterial agent like *bordatella bronchiseptica*, or by a virus like parainfluenza.

Overall, there are three viruses and at least six strains of bacteria that can work in combination to cause kennel cough in a dog's respiratory system. Secondary bacterial infections can also be present, and it is possible for kennel cough to progress to pneumonia in some cases.

Although bordatella is considered "zoonotic," meaning it can be transferred from dogs to humans, the data regarding humans contracting bronchitis from their pets is contradictory at best. If this transmission were to occur, it would most likely affect the very young, the very old, or anyone with a compromised immune system.

Kennel cough may be passed to other companion animals, however, including cats. Having the disease once does not convey immunity against future infections, and recovered dogs with no symptoms may remain contagious for lengthy periods of time.

When inhaled, the disease-causing microorganisms attach themselves to the moist lining of the animal's trachea (wind pipe) and upper airways. There, the organisms begin to grow, damaging the cells they infect.

Dogs with this form of bronchitis have a dry, hacking cough that may be accompanied by dry heaving and a thin discharge from the nose. In older dogs or those with an existing health condition, lethargy and fever may be present.

Most cases of kennel cough resolve in 7 to 10 days without treatment. If medications are used, they are typically aimed at relieving the animal's cough with some type of suppressant, often an over-the-counter formula recommended by a veterinarian. Antibiotics are only needed if fever is present or a secondary bacterial agent is suspected.

There are other health conditions in dogs, however, that can present with a cough in their early stages. It's a mistake to simply assume that your pet has kennel cough.

While it is impossible to prevent kennel cough completely, its prevalence makes it important for all dog owners to understand the condition and to understand what they can do to at least minimize the risk that their pet will be infected.

Acknowledgements

I would like to express my gratitude towards my family, friends, and colleagues for their kind co-operation and encouragement which helped me in completion of this book.

I would like to express my special gratitude and thanks to my loving husband for his patience, understanding, and support.

My thanks and appreciations also go to my colleagues and people who have willingly helped me out with their abilities.

Additional thanks to my children, whose love and care for our family pets inspired me to write this book.

Table of Contents

Table of Contents

Part 1 - Introduction to Kennel Cough

There are many myths about kennel cough, a disease feared by uninformed dog owners as a fatal condition.

While certainly highly contagious, the idea that kennel cough is a death sentence stems from the fact that when animals in rescue shelters contract the infection, they are often euthanized as "too sick to adopt."

It cannot be stressed strongly enough that this is a decision based on matters of budget and space, *not* a medical necessity.

Rescue and shelter groups are chronically strapped for funds. Placement of homeless animals is already difficult. Very few people will take a dog that is sick, even with something as treatable as kennel cough.

Faced with the prospect of feeding, housing, and treating the infected animal for weeks with already limited funds, most facilities opt to tragically "solve" the problem another way.

Truthfully, most cases of kennel cough resolve on their own in under two weeks and the animal recovers fully.

Increasing the level of public awareness about the true nature of kennel cough will not only help existing pet owners to safeguard the health of their beloved companions, but it may also support better solutions for shelter dogs.

One of the most vital functions animal welfare volunteers can provide to shelters is to step forward as foster families for dogs suffering from kennel cough.

Removing sick animals from the shelter environment for the duration of the recovery period not only saves the life of the individual dog, but also lessens the chance of the infection spreading throughout the broader shelter population.

When the affected dogs are fully recovered and past the stage when they remain contagious, they are completely adoptable. There are no long-term consequences of kennel cough. For the vast majority of dogs, it is really no worse than a common cold in humans.

Currently, the popular perception of kennel cough swings between two extremes, however, a death sentence and "nothing to worry about."
The reality of the disease lies in the middle ground where informed education can make all the difference in the world, both for worried owners and for the dogs they love. That is the purpose of this book.

What is kennel cough?

Kennel cough is an infectious respiratory disease seen most often in dogs. It can be contracted by other companion species, including cats, but those instances are more rare.

The scientific name for kennel cough is canine infectious tracheobronchitis. Puppies age 6 weeks to 6 months are particularly vulnerable, but a dog of any age can come down with this illness.

There is no conveyed immunity following a bout of kennel cough, so a dog can have it more than once during their lives, just as humans suffer periodically from colds and upper respiratory infections.

A combination of simultaneous infectious agents can be responsible for a case of kennel cough. The major viral causes are, in order of prevalence:

- canine parainfluenza virus
- canine adenovirus 2 (canine distemper virus)
- canine adenovirus 1

Bacterial agents prominent in kennel cough infections include:

- bordetella bronchiseptica (the most common)
- streptococcus
- pasteurella
- pseudomonas
- e. coli
- mycoplasma

It is highly debatable whether kennel cough is zoonotic, meaning that humans can catch it from their companion animals.

Bordetella bronchiseptica is zoonotic on rare occasions in very young children, the elderly, or individuals with a compromised immune system.

Kennel cough is, however, simply a form of bronchitis, which is contagious, so in theory, it could be passed to humans. It is more likely that if a human were to be infected from a dog it would be via a bacterial agent rather than a virus, but there is no evidence to suggest this is the case.

A dog with kennel cough can pass the infection to cats, rabbits, pigs and guinea pigs, but this occurs only rarely.

Kennel Cough vs. Distemper

There is a popular tendency to confuse kennel cough with canine distemper, which is a much more serious condition.

Calloway County Public Library
710 Main Street
Murray, Kentucky 42071
(270) 753-2288
www.callowaycountylibrary.org

This is a huge misconception. The two illnesses are NOT the same, nor do they have the same prognosis.

Most cases of kennel cough are bacterial in nature, while a virus is the root cause of distemper. The distemper infection does begin in the respiratory system, but then goes on to attack the gastrointestinal and nervous systems, and the conjunctival membranes in the eyes.

Canine distemper initially presents with coughing and sneezing. However, there will be thick, yellow discharge from the eyes and nose. The dog will rapidly develop a fever, become lethargic, and experience both vomiting and diarrhea. Marked depression and loss of appetite are also present.

Dogs with distemper get very sick very quickly. The disease is highly contagious, passing through direct contact with urine, blood, and saliva. Dogs that share food and water bowls are particularly vulnerable, and the virus can be airborne via coughing and sneezing.

Any time it is suspected that a dog has a case of distemper, the aid of a veterinarian must be sought immediately. The disease is aggressive and often deadly. Puppies and adolescent dogs that have not yet been vaccinated are the most vulnerable to distemper.

Currently, there is no medicine that will directly destroy the virus that causes this illness. Treatment involves supportive care including antibiotics to prevent secondary infections as well as the administration of intravenous fluids for dehydration.

It is difficult to predict the outcome of a case of distemper. Even some dogs who seem at the brink of death rally and recover. Others die very quickly. (Note that distemper is also present in cats, and is equally virulent in that species.)

Distemper and kennel cough are NOT the same condition. Dogs with kennel cough do not display the crippling lethargy and loss of appetite common in cases of distemper. If they have a discharge from the eyes or nose it tends to be clear and watery.

If your dog is sneezing and coughing, and if a discolored, thick discharge is present, immediately take the animal to a veterinarian. Only a qualified vet can determine the true nature of the animal's illness and prescribe the proper treatment.

How does kennel cough typically occur?

Kennel cough is transmitted from one infected dog to another through microscopic water vapor or particles of dust. Basically the dog "sprays" the virus into the air around him. If another dog is present, the infectious agents are inhaled.

It is not known how long the viruses and bacteria that are primarily responsible for kennel cough can live on surfaces in the environment. For this reason, thoroughly cleaning and disinfecting an area where an infected dog is present is one of the primary means of defense against the disease spreading.

This is also the reason that veterinary clinics, grooming facilities, and boarding kennels should routinely wipe down all surfaces with which multiple dogs come into contact. All individuals working in these places should disinfect their hands after handling one dog and before touching another.

When a dog inhales the kennel cough infectious agent, the organisms attach themselves to the lining of the trachea and the upper airways leading to the lungs. There, the organisms replicate on the moist surface of the organs, damaging adjoining cells as they grow.

The spread of the disease is extremely common in any closed environment where multiple dogs are present, for instance a kennel, animal shelter, or a dog show. A single infected dog can be the source of a widespread outbreak.

This is true no matter how well the environment is ventilated, how large the space might be, and how well it is cleaned and maintained. One of the most frustrating things about kennel cough is how difficult it is to prevent infections.

Dogs that have recently recovered from kennel cough may remain infectious for weeks after their symptoms disappear. Additionally, a dog that has had kennel cough once is not immune from contracting the condition a second time.

Is kennel cough seasonal?

Although kennel cough can occur at any time of year, veterinarians see more cases during the warm summer months for the simple reason that more people go away on vacation at that time and tend to board their animals.

Even if a family opts to take Rover along on summer vacation, the dog's risk of exposure to kennel cough still becomes elevated. Coming into contact with strange dogs at campgrounds and other family vacation spots is an open invitation for kennel cough to be transmitted to your pet.

This is not only because other dogs may be carrying the virus. Your dog's immune system can be weakened by the stress and excitement of the trip itself. Both humans and dogs are vulnerable to coming down with a vacation "bug" for this reason.

How does kennel cough present?

About 3 to 7 days after infection occurs, the following major symptoms will begin to present in an infected dog:
- A dry hacking cough that sounds coarse, as if the animal were trying to clear its throat.
- Dry heaving, as if the dog were trying to get something up out of its throat.
- A thin, runny discharge from the nose.

Many dogs will cough every few minutes for the duration of the infection. They remain alert and active and continue to eat, but their coughing is constant.

In older dogs, or those that are immunocompromised, the animal may become lethargic and run a fever. In these cases, the risk of the infection progressing to pneumonia is very high, and in some rare cases, death may result.

What is the duration and treatment of kennel cough?

In the absence of any complications, the symptoms of kennel cough typically resolve in 7-10 days, but the condition may persist for as long as three weeks.

Treatment typically focuses on relieving the dog's discomfort with cough suppressants — generally a pediatric or other over-the-counter formulation recommended by your veterinarian.

If the animal has a fever or if secondary bacterial agents are present, prescription cough medication may be required and antibiotics are typically prescribed.

Part 2 - Understanding Kennel Cough In-Depth

All pet owners understand the frustration of living with a highly intelligent creature that can't tell us exactly how it feels. Your dog's preventive health care is entirely in your hands, and must be tinged with a bit of mind reading.

When your pet has a cough, it's a mistake to assume anything. Only a veterinarian can make an accurate diagnosis of any health condition in your dog.

You can, however, go into the situation armed with enough knowledge to ask the right questions and to assimilate the answers, translating them into the actions that will best help your canine companion.

A Word on Working with a Veterinarian

The average dog owner spends approximately $655 / £427 a year on health care for their pet, an increase of 50% over the last decade. The cost of treating a routine case of kennel cough is roughly $100-$150 / £65/£98.

However, if the disease is misdiagnosed or progresses to pneumonia, those costs will escalate rapidly. If, for instance, you dog's cough were to turn out to be a case of heartworm, the treatment protocol runs 3-4 months at a conservative estimate of $1000-$2000 / £652-£1304.

A typical vet visit to evaluate your dog's condition starts at around $50 / £33. If your pet needs nothing more than an over-the-counter cough suppressant, you'll be out about $5-$7 / £3.26-£4.56 a bottle.

Although the kennel cough vaccine, which guards only against infection from the bacteria *bordatella bronchiseptica* is controversial, it is also relatively inexpensive, ranging from $25-$75 / £16-£50 depending on your veterinarian.

With a condition like kennel cough, you are not only taking good care of your pet by immediately having the dog checked out by a veterinarian, you are being financially smart.

Guessing about your dog's health or waiting to see if the animal gets better on its own is not only potentially dangerous for the dog, but potentially expensive for you.

If your dog is coughing, take the animal to the vet!

The Canine Respiratory System

In basic terms, a dog's respiratory system, like our own, is divided into upper and lower tracts. The upper tract consists of the:

- nose
- nasal sinuses
- throat
- trachea

The lower tract is comprised of the bronchi or bronchioles, also known as the "small airways," and alveoli, which are air sacs embedded in lung tissue. They are responsible for oxygen exchange.

Kennel cough affects the upper respiratory system, with the infectious agents embedding themselves in the moist tissues of the airways.

If the infection progresses to pneumonia, the lower respiratory tract becomes involved.

The Severity of Kennel Cough

Most cases of kennel cough resolve without treatment in under two weeks. Medications like antibiotics and cough suppressants may speed recovery and make the animal more comfortable, but the infection will have to run its course. The animal should be confined for at least a week after all symptoms have disappeared.

It is important, however, not to simply assume that if your dog is coughing, kennel cough is the reason. Only a vet can accurately evaluate the nature of any illness, and there are a number of conditions that present with a cough that must be ruled out for the safety of your pet.

When to See a Vet

If your dog's symptoms persist for more than a week, and if any of the following additional symptoms are present individually or collectively, it is imperative that you take your animal to a veterinarian:

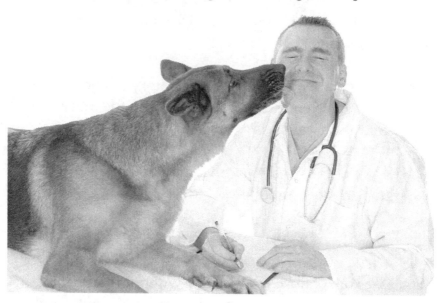

- Thick nasal discharge that is either yellow or green.
- Rapid respiration.
- Loss of appetite.
- Lethargy.

Your pet may be suffering from a more serious condition. Remember, kennel cough itself can turn into a life-threatening case of pneumonia.

Diseases and Conditions with Similar Symptoms

A number of conditions in dogs present with coughing. Many are life threatening, and should not be ignored. Some of the more common of these illnesses include the following.

Blastomycocis

Blastomycocis is a potentially fatal, yeast-like fungal infection in dogs caused by *Blastomyces dermatitidis*. It is contracted when the animal comes into contact with decaying wood and soil, which places sporting breeds at an especially high risk.

The fungus thrives in damp, moist environments like swamps, lakes, and riverbeds. Any place where direct sunlight does not reach the soil to dry it out is a fertile breeding ground for *Blastomyces dermatitidis*.

Studies have determined that most dogs that contract blastomycocis live within 450 yards (412 meters) of some body of water.

In the United States, the fungus is found most often in Mississippi, Ohio, Missouri, and the Tennessee River basin as well as in the central and southeastern states. There have, however, been documented cases of Blastomycocis in companion dogs in Canada, India, Israel, Saudi Arabia, and Africa.

In the lungs, the *Blastomyces dermatitidis* spores bud into a large, thick-walled growth of yeast that multiples rapidly. The symptoms of the condition include coughing and wheezing, but one of the most serious consequences can be permanent blindness if the infection spreads to the eyes.

In the early stages, Blastomycocis can sound like kennel cough. As it progresses, however, the animal will experience loss of appetite with accompanying weight loss, skin lesions, eye infections, swollen lymph glands, and joint pain among other effects.

A Blastomycocis infection is not zoonotic; it cannot be spread from a dog to a human, or from a human to a dog. Although humans who inhale the spores rarely become ill, when they do, the symptoms of the condition are flu-like in nature and typically present 3-15 weeks after exposure.

Valley Fever

Valley Fever or Coccidioidomycosis is a non-contagious pulmonary fungal infection in dogs and other domestic animals. The illness begins in the lungs where the inhaled spores of *Coccidioides immitis* grow after having been inhaled from soil containing the fungus.

In infected dogs, the lymph nodes near the heart become swollen as the disease progresses and press against the windpipe causing a cough that can sound like early stage kennel cough. If the infection spreads beyond the lungs and becomes disseminated, the fungus attacks the leg bones causing lameness and swelling.

Additional symptoms include soft swellings under the skin, non-healing skin ulcerations, inflammation of the eyes, swollen testicles in males, and seizures.

Valley Fever outbreaks tend to occur primarily in the low desert regions of Arizona, New Mexico, and southwestern Texas.

Approximately 70% of dogs that come into contact with the fungus spores have no reaction. The remainder of those exposed have mild to severe cases of the illness. Occasionally the disease is fatal due to sudden heart failure.

A proper diagnosis of Valley Fever requires blood tests, and the treatment of choice is the oral antifungal drug, Fluconazole.

Note that Valley Fever is zoonotic. In humans it presents with a fever, cough, chest pain (a restrictive feeling or a sense of pressure resembling a heart attack), chills, night sweats, headache, fatigue, aching joints and a red (spotty) rash.

Heartworms

Heartworm disease is spread by mosquitoes and is thus found in dogs living throughout the world. The larva of a parasitic worm (*Dirofilaria immitis*) enters the dog's system through the mosquito bite. Six months later, the adult worm has traveled to and becomes lodged in the right side of the heart.

The earliest symptoms of heartworm are a tendency to fatigue easily, intolerance for any kind of exercise, and a deep cough.

As the disease progresses the animal loses weight, experiences rapid and labored breathing, and may suffer from a bulging of the chest.

Cases of heartworm that are not treated will cause permanent damage to the heart, lungs, liver, and kidneys, and will eventually prove fatal.

Cardiac Disease

Virtually all canine cardiac disease can present with a persistent cough. This may be due to enlargement of the heart or of the surrounding lymph nodes, or even an accompanying decrease in oxygen levels in the blood.

One of the most common cardiac complaints leading to coughing is congestive heart failure. Backpressure in the blood vessels from the lungs to the heart causes fluid to leak into the lungs.

The cough is the body's way of trying to clear the lungs. Typically a diuretic will be prescribed to facilitate fluid removal via the kidneys.

Over time, however, the chambers of the heart may become enlarged, in particular the right atrium. If the enlargement is severe, the heart presses against the main stem bronchus, which supplies air to the lungs.

Again, coughing is the body's natural response. At this stage of congestive heart disease, there is really no way to eliminate the cough.

Many dogs live for years on proper cardiac medication, but it is imperative that the given condition be diagnosed early.

It is vital to rule out an underlying heart problem as the cause of any persistent cough in a dog.

Reverse Sneezing in Toy Breeds

Reverse sneezing or pharyngeal gag reflex is a condition often seen in toy breeds. It happens frequently after the animal has been drinking water, is excited, or when the animal is subjected to a sudden change in temperature, like going outside on a cold winter day.

The dog will make wheezing and hacking sounds, sometimes accompanied by snorting. The reaction is caused when air passes back and forth quickly and dramatically through the nasal passages. It is worse if the dog has a mild throat irritation.

Owners can grow quite alarmed by reverse sneezing, however, since the dog will take long, fast breaths. Affected dogs tend to stand with their legs widely planted, necks extended, and their eyes may bulge or open wide from the effort of clearing their breathing.

The duration of the incident is rarely more than a minute or two, and gently rubbing the dog's throat will help to ease the spasms. It is also helpful to lightly block the dog's nose holes, forcing it to breath through its mouth. For those few seconds, however, the common reaction humans have is the fear that their pet is choking to death.

If reverse sneezing is chronic, some owners – and even vets -- have the mistaken belief that their animals are suffering from chronic kennel cough. In reverse sneezing, however, there is no pathogen present. The dog is simply suffering from a different kind of gag reflex.

Collapsed Trachea in Toy Breeds

The trachea, more commonly called the "windpipe," is a tube protected by cartilaginous "rings" that do not completely encircle the structure. In smaller dog breeds, if the cartilage is not stiff enough to keep the trachea open, the tube can collapse or flatten during rapid inhalation.

The condition is seen most often in Chihuahuas, Maltese, Shih Tzus, Pomeranians, Yorkies, Lhasa Apsos, pugs, and toy poodles. The trait may be genetic and a consequence of breeders manipulating their bloodlines to achieve smaller physical sizes.

Dogs with the condition experience a chronic, harsh cough that is often mistaken for kennel cough. The animals tend to cough more during the day, but less at night. Episodes will be worse when the dog is excited, or when it's drinking water.

One way to distinguish a case of collapsed trachea from kennel cough is the sound of the cough itself. If the problem is the structure of the trachea rather than an infection, the dog will sound more like a goose honking. Kennel cough sounds almost as if the dog is trying to clear its throat.

With collapsed trachea, over time, the trachea begins to weaken. Then, the coughing episodes may last for several minutes. In older dogs, the symptoms can become severe enough to warrant medication.

Contributing factors that will worsen cases of collapsed trachea include obesity, allergies, concurrent heart issues, and smoking by the pet owner.

Dogs prone to collapsed trachea are more susceptible to develop bacterial and viral infections, so it is possible for a dog to have both a collapsed trachea *and* suffer a bout of kennel cough. Only a veterinarian can determine the true nature of the complaint.

X-rays will be required, and a scope outfitted with a camera may be introduced into the throat while the animal is under anesthesia to more accurately observe the condition of the trachea.

Canine Influenza

It is easy to become confused by the terms "canine parainfluenza" and "canine influenza."

Canine parainfluenza is a virus commonly referred to as CPIV and is one of the most common infectious agents leading to kennel cough.

Canine influenza is a distinct illness caused by various strains of influenzavirus A including the equine influenza virus H3N8 to which dogs have no natural immunity.

Approximately 80% of dogs infected display mild symptoms, but the illness is rarely fatal. Symptoms last from 10 to 30 days and include a cough and a green nasal discharge. In severe cases, fever and pneumonia will be present.

As is the case with kennel cough, dogs with canine influenza that develop pneumonia are at a much higher risk of death (about 50%).

Potential Complications of Kennel Cough

Complications from kennel cough surface most often in puppies, elderly dogs, and immunosuppressed individuals.

The greatest potential is for the condition to progress to pneumonia, which, if untreated, can prove fatal.

Secondary bacterial infections are also a possibility because the small hairs or cilia of the respiratory tract will have been damaged or destroyed during the course of the illness.

This may trigger an increase in the body's immune response leading to a buildup of mucus, which in turn blocks the sinuses and leads to a secondary infection.

Should such an infection spread to the lungs, pneumonia will likely result. As fluid builds up in the lungs, oxygen flow to the bloodstream is compromised.

Any series of complications accompanying kennel cough raises the potential for the dog to go into shock and die.

Always listen closely to the nature of your animal's cough. With normal cases of kennel cough, the sound is dry and coarse. If pneumonia is present, the cough will be wet and heavy.

Understanding the Kennel Cough Vaccine

The "kennel cough" vaccine is actually an injection or nasal mist that specifically targets the bacteria *bordetella bronchiseptica*, which is only one of several potential infectious agents underlying canine infectious tracheobronchitis.

Because bordetella is a very common cause of kennel cough, however, this vaccine is required by the vast majority of canine day care, grooming, and boarding facilities.

(Note that when the vaccine is administered as an intranasal mist it will be four days before the dog enjoys any protection. If injected, it is not effective for seven days.)

Kennel Cough Vaccine is Controversial

Detractors of the kennel cough vaccine argue that the requirement for the vaccine is meaningless, and even potentially dangerous.

In a small percentage of cases (less than 5%), some dogs will develop kennel cough 3-10 days after being given the vaccine. In rare cases, dogs have gone into anaphylactic shock within minutes.

With any vaccination, it's best to ask the vet to allow you to remain at the clinic until you are certain your dog is not going to have a life-threatening reaction.

A dog's system changes over time, so do not assume that simply because your dog has never had a problem with a vaccine that issues cannot arise in the future.

Typically 30 minutes is sufficient time to gauge your dog's reaction. If the clinic is crowded and busy, remain in the waiting room or parking lot. The point is to have access to emergency help if you need it.

Even proponents of the kennel cough vaccine acknowledge that when given as a shot, the vaccine can raise a sore lump at the injection site. Other side effects may include hives, lethargy, vomiting, diarrhea, and difficulty breathing.

Armed with this information, many owners ask what does seem to be a reasonable question. "Why should I risk vaccinating my dog against a disease that is not life threatening?"

The principle objection to the vaccine is much more basic, however. It provides only partial protection from one of many infectious agents that may cause kennel cough. Additionally, the vaccine will do nothing to relieve the symptoms of an animal that has already contracted the infection.

For owners who object to the kennel cough vaccine, options for grooming and boarding have to be re-examined. There are groomers who will come to your home, and you can hire a pet sitter to feed and water your pet when you are away.

Typically these services are more expensive as they involve travel costs for the provider. Dogs that suffer from separation anxiety may become destructive when left home alone. Certainly there are combination pet and house sitters, but you are then faced with the prospect of finding someone you trust to be in your home.

There are always down sides to either approach, but in truth, the only way to effectively protect your pet against kennel cough and other infectious diseases is to limit or eliminate your pet's exposure to other animals.

If you add to this a reluctance to vaccinate, "at home" options for grooming and care are all that remain.

Best Medications for Kennel Cough

Most cases of kennel cough are treated symptomatically. It is common for the vet to recommend some form of cough suppressant, turning to antibiotics if the dog begins to run a fever, or is not eating well.

Over-the-Counter Medications

Dextromethorphan (commonly sold as Robitussin-DM) is frequently used to treat kennel cough, but should only be administered under the guidance of a veterinarian. The product helps to lessen airway irritation and will loosen and dislodge mucus that is present.

The drug is not approved for veterinary use, although it is accepted practice. It works to suppress the cough center of the brain, and does not have the sedative effect of narcotic cough suppressants.

If you are giving your dog dextromethorphan and the animal becomes nauseous and vomits, or shows signs of dizziness or drowsiness, discontinue use of the product and consult your veterinarian.

Do NOT simply assume that your dog has kennel cough and give the animal an over-the-counter cough suppressant without direction from a vet. In dogs with a productive, moist cough it is important that the animal's body get rid of the phlegm and secretions in the lungs.

NEVER use any medication with a dog that includes acetaminophen, caffeine, or alcohol. All can be deadly to pets.

Expect to pay approximately $5-$7 / £3.26-£4.56 a bottle for a dextromethorphan cough suppressant.

Veterinary Prescriptions

There are a variety of medications your vet may prescribe to relieve the discomfort your dog experiences from kennel cough symptoms. These include, but are not limited to:

- Temaril-P, a mixture of trimeprazine (an antihistamine) and prednisolone (a corticosteroid to reduce inflammation.) The medication is administered as a pill with food and may cause drowsiness. The cost is approximately $1 / £0.65 per pill.

Some dogs are allergic to Temaril-P. The medication should not be given to dogs that are pregnant or those with diabetes.

Allergic reactions are characterized by labored breathing, oral and facial swelling, and hives. Other adverse symptoms may include, but are not limited to, tremors and

35

muscle weakness, increased thirst, urination, hunger, vomiting, and diarrhea.

Temaril-P should not be given in combination with herbal products, sedatives, anesthetics, pain medications, epinephrine, and procaine.

- Sulfamethoxazole and Trimethroprim taken in combination are affective against a wide range of bacterial infections. Sulfamethoxazole is an antibiotic that inhibits bacterial growth, while trimethoprim deprives bacteria of the nucleotides required for DNA replication. The mixture is given orally once a day at a cost of approximately $0.40 / £0.26 per tablet.

These drugs are not appropriate for pregnant or nursing animals. They may increase your dog's sensitivity to sunlight.

In dogs experiencing an allergic reaction swelling of the mouth and face can occur, and hives are also a possibility. Watch for bleeding or bruising, and any yellowing of the eyes.

Other adverse reactions may include nausea and dizziness, vomiting, decreased appetite, diarrhea, fatigue, and weakness.

- Clavamox, which is a broad-spectrum antibiotic combining amoxicillin and chavulanic acid. It is used primarily to treat infections caused by bacteria and can be administered as a tablet or a liquid. The cost per tablet is approximately $0.80 / £0.52 with a 15ml bottle selling for around $30 / £20.

If your dog experiences diarrhea while taking Clavamox, immediately contact your veterinarian. Allergic reactions to this medication can include fainting, the presence of a rash, hives and swelling of the lips, tongue, and face.

- Baytril, a fluoroquinolone antibiotic that addresses bacterial infections by interfering with bacterial DNA metabolism. It is administered as a tablet at a cost of $1.75-$5.00 / £1.14-£3.26 per pill depending on strength.
If your dog displays a depressed appetite, vomiting, diarrhea, dizziness, or drowsiness while taking Baytril, contact your vet at once. Allergic reactions can include difficulty breathing, swelling of the face and mouth, and hives.

Natural Remedies for Kennel Cough

Since treatment of kennel cough tends to focus strongly on the relief of symptoms, many owners opt for natural remedies to help their dogs, especially if the animal remains alert, active, and is eating well in spite of the persistent cough.

(Note that the dosages listed below are calculated for a 10 lb. / 4.53 kg dog. Almost all of the herbs are available in health food stores in capsule form for less than $10 / £6.52 a bottle. To administer, break open the capsule and mix the powder in food or a treat.)

- Echinacea: Echinacea administered once daily with food (125 mg) has proven to be effective in cases of kennel cough caused by the bordetella bacteria.

- Vitamin C and E: Both Vitamin C and E have antiviral properties and can provide powerful support to the immune system. Administer 500 mg once a day of each vitamin after the dog's regular meal.

- Oregano Oil: Oregano oil is a multi-purpose natural remedy that has antiseptic, antifungal, antiviral, and antibacterial properties. Simply dribble a small amount over your dog's food, wet or dry.
- Astragalus: An herb used widely in Chinese medicine, astragalus boosts the immune system while supporting lung function and stimulating the regrowth of bronchial cells. When used for kennel cough, it is typically purchased as a liquid (tincture) and administered at a rate of one drop per 1 lb. / 0.45 kg of the animal's weight.

- Raw Garlic: While raw garlic is a natural antibacterial and antiviral agent, it should be noted that not all dogs tolerate eating it. Many experience gastrointestinal distress when fed garlic, so proceed with caution and discontinue use immediately if your dog exhibits any stomach-related symptoms including flatulence.

(If this is the case, you may try the powder from one 500 mg garlic powder administered once a day.)

- Raw honey: Raw honey goes a long way toward soothing the discomfort your dog will experience from the persistent

38

hacking cough that goes along with this disease. Most dogs have a bit of a sweet tooth anyway, so it's quite simple to get them to lick a spoonful of honey. Dispense as needed.

- Essential Oils: Essential oils are not given as a medication per se, but can be used on the dog's bedding, or simply held near the animal's nose to help open up the breathing passages. Eucalyptus, lavender, tea tree, and chamomile oils all have decongestant and calming properties. Use as needed. (These may also be added to a vaporizer placed in proximity to where your pet sleeps.)

- Slippery Elm: This herb can help to soothe throat irritation. Buy the herb in capsule form and mix with honey and water to make a "lickable" syrup. Most dogs regard the mixture as a treat and will take it readily.

Keeping the air moist with either a vaporizer or humidifier is one of the best measures you can take to ease you dog's discomfort from kennel cough. Both will help to open the animal's bronchial tubes and clear phlegm from the throat.

It's also a good idea to turn on the shower and let the bathroom fill with steam. Stay in the room with your dog for 15-20 minutes to allow for the full benefit of the "treatment."

Kennel Cough Recovery Tips

Unless complications arise, kennel cough is a "watchful waiting" type of illness. Monitor your dog's behavior and consult your veterinarian immediately if the coughing increases in either intensity or frequency.

If your dog routinely wears a collar, remove it so there is no constriction against the animal's throat. Since kennel cough is highly contagious, you will want to keep your dog indoors and away from other animals for at least a week after all symptoms have resolved.

Again, the primary focus is on symptom relief. If your dog is active, alert, and eating well, both you and he will simply have to wait out the persistent hacking cough.

Keep especially exuberant dogs as calm and contained as possible, since running and strenuous activity can make the coughing worse. Also, try not to let your dog get wet or cold while he is recovering from his illness.

When Kennel Cough Becomes Pneumonia

Pneumonia in dogs is often preceded by an upper respiratory infection like kennel cough. Although any dog can have pneumonia, puppies and older animals are in the highest risk category followed by individuals with a compromised immune system, a chronic illness, or those that have received chemotherapy.

Bacterial pneumonia is common in dogs that suffer from a collapsing trachea or chronic bronchitis. It can also be caused by the presence of foreign bodies in the lower airway, typically from inhalation, aspiration, or reflux.

The major symptoms of pneumonia are rapid breathing, coughing, fever, depression, and a racing pulse. A thick nasal discharge may be present. Sometimes dogs with pneumonia will extend their heads and sit with their elbows pointed outward in an effort to expand the chest.

The sound of the dog's cough will be moist and bubbling. Cough suppressants should not be used because the dog needs to clear its airways to make breathing easier. The animal will require immediate veterinary care, starting with a chest X-ray to confirm the diagnosis of pneumonia.

The vet will prescribe an antibiotic to be administered for a minimum of three weeks or until such time as the chest and lungs are clear on an X-ray.

Projected Treatment Costs

Although prices vary widely by veterinary practice, the initial consultation visit regardless of the final diagnosis should cost around $50 / £33.

Nasal swabs to test for the presence of disease causing agents typically cost $30-$40 / £20-£26.

Once a diagnosis of kennel cough is made, you will likely need little more than an over-the-counter cough syrup or a homemade remedy. Both can be made or obtained for $10 / £6.5 or less.

In simple cases of kennel cough then, you're looking at roughly $100 / £65 in treatment costs. Should the dog develop pneumonia, expect that cost to double, at minimum.

Part 3 – Preventing and Managing Kennel Cough

It is important to understand that kennel cough can never be totally prevented. The condition is highly contagious. One infected animal can be the source of a widespread outbreak in any environment where multiple dogs are present.

An owner's best option for protecting a dog against kennel cough or any infectious disease is to concentrate on keeping the animal's immune system as strong possible.

Strengthening Your Dog's Immune System

Your dog's immune system is a complex interaction of biochemical processes designed to protect the animal's body from parasites, bacteria, fungus, and viruses. The stronger the dog's immune system, the better able he will be to fight off these natural microorganisms, as well as any toxins with which he comes into contact.

Not only will you be helping your dog to stay ahead of kennel cough, you will also be protecting him from chronic yeast and fungal infections, eczema, food allergies, arthritis, and ear infections among other conditions. Additionally, strong immune systems boost wound healing.

A Well-Balanced Diet

The first line of defense in a solid immune system is a good diet. Commercial dog foods vary widely in quality, and thus in price. It's a constant balancing act to find a food that gives your pet everything he needs and fits your budget.

Beyond these facts, however, there are now specialized diets available to manage specific diseases, to circumvent allergic reactions, and to accommodate level of activity, rate of growth, reproductive status, age, and environmental conditions.

For instance a puppy that lives indoors will require different nutrition than a sporting dog that works outside or a nursing female. You are always best advised to first discuss your dog's nutritional needs with your veterinarian, or, if you have a purebred animal, with your breeder.

There are, however, some general guidelines you can follow in selecting food for your dog. Always read the list of ingredients and make sure that meat is the first item mentioned. If the first ingredient is corn, move on.

The optimum ratio for a healthy diet in most dogs is 50% meat and 50% vegetables with no cheap filler grains or wheat.

Foods that are high in omega fatty acids boost the production of energy in the body and aid in food utilization.

Try to buy products with minimal amounts of artificial colorings and preservatives. Chemicals won't make your dog healthier. In particular you want to avoid the preservatives BHA, BHT, and Ethoxyquin.

BHA is the abbreviation for butylated hydroxyanisole. It has been consistently linked to tumor production in animals.

BHT or butylated hydroxytoluene has likewise been linked to cancer. (The fact that it is an ingredient in embalming fluid is enough for most people to want to avoid it for either their dogs or themselves.)

Ethoxyquin is used as a hardening agent in the manufacture of rubber and as a pesticide in addition to its role as a preservative in dog food. The chemical has been linked to birth defects in puppies, still births, liver failure, infertility, and cancer.

At the same time that you're concentrating on feeding your dog well, keep him well hydrated. A constant source of clean drinking water helps your dog to flush toxins out of his system before they can do any damage.

Plenty of Exercise

Far too many dogs, especially those living in the city, are unnaturally sedentary. Get your pet out to the park or hiking trails and really give him a workout tossing a ball or a stick.

Sunshine is an excellent source of Vitamin D3, which contributes to strong bone health, and the exercise pumps lots of good, fresh oxygen throughout your pet's system.

But perhaps even more important is the role of exercise in combatting stress. Dogs that are cooped up all the time become chronically anxious. This is one of the reasons dogs in shelters are so vulnerable to kennel cough.

They are being kept in a confined space with too much noise and too much light. They're afraid, and they're not getting enough interaction. All dogs need exercise, but especially if you've just adopted a shelter dog, get him outside on a leash and play with him!

Not only is this an excellent way to bond, it will immeasurably help the dog's health.

Supplements for Immunity

Don't rule out the use of supplements to boost your dog's immunity, but always discuss such a program with your vet first.

Two herbs you may want to consider that specifically target the immune system are milk thistle and dandelion. Both come in capsule form and neither is toxic, so simply break open a capsule and mix it with your dog's food.

A typical size capsule is 250 mg. Judge dosage by bowel tolerance. If your dog's stools become loose, discontinue the herb for a day or two and then resume at a lower dosage. (One hundred 250 mg capsules of either herb sells for approximately $6-$8 / £4-£6. Note that since milk thistle is also good for liver disease, it can be purchased in liquid form for dogs. A 2 oz. bottle, which is roughly a one-month supply costs approximately $35 / £23.)

Many dog owners swear by Vitamin C powder, which can be sprinkled on the dog's food or even mixed with its water provided the animal finds the taste agreeable.

A product like Halo VitaGlo Xtra-C Vitamin C Powder Pet Supplement offers 4,000 mg per teaspoon. As an example of dosage, 1/16 to 1/8 of a teaspoon (0.62 / 0.12 tsp UK) is recommended for dogs weighing 2-11 lbs. (1-5.5 kg). Expect to pay $28 / £18.45 per 8 oz. / 226 grams.

If you choose to go the multi-vitamin route for your pet, look for a canine-specific product like Only Natural Pet Super Daily Canine Multi-Vitamins, which sell for approximately $30 / £19.7 for 270 tablets.

The tablets can be given whole, or crushed in food. They should not, however, be cooked, as the heat will destroy the vitamin content. Dispense 1 table for dogs of up to 20 lbs. (9 kg) and 2 for dogs 20-70 lbs. (9-32 kg).

The water-soluble vitamins dogs need daily include:

- Vitamin C
- Vitamin B1
- Vitamin B2
- Vitamin B3
- Vitamin B5
- Vitamin B6
- Vitamin B12

- Folic Acid
- Biotin

As dogs age, they absorb fewer vitamins and minerals in their intestinal tract, and may require more supplementation than younger dogs, including fat-soluble vitamins like A and E.

Probiotics for Healthier Digestion

Probiotic therapy has already proven to immeasurably help dogs with chronic diarrhea, inflammatory bowel disease, pancreatitis, and chronic renal diseases. The latest research indicates, however, that probiotics will also strengthen a pet's immune system by achieving proper digestive balance.

A dog's digestive tract is actually his largest immune organ. The intestinal tract is full of bacteria and is designed to handle a large bacterial load. If, however, "bad" bacteria overwhelms a dog's intestinal tract, he becomes much more susceptible to all manner of illnesses.

Probiotics are, simply put, "good bacteria" that are introduced into your dog's diet in powder form. When eaten, they efficiently re-colonize in the digestive tract where they aid in digestion and food absorption.

Eight ounces (227 grams) of probiotic powder (enough for up to 120 servings) sells for approximately $25 / £16.5.

Do Not Neglect Preventive Medicine

The truth is that most people take better care of their dogs than they do of themselves, so chances are good your pet is already seeing a vet routinely. If not, get your dog on a schedule of once-a-year wellness checks.

In addition to keeping the animal current with its vaccines, these visits help the vet to get an overall sense of the dog's health and to spot potential problems before they become serious.

For instance, poor dental health and a build-up of bacteria in the mouth is one of the leading causes of heart disease in companion animals.

Having a vet look at your dog's teeth once a year will ensure the animal is getting good dental care and that the window is not being opened for any opportunistic infection – including kennel cough – to enter his system.

Exercise Caution Around Other Dogs

Although no one wants to keep dogs in complete isolation, the only reasonably guaranteed way to guard against kennel cough is to do just that.

Arrange "play dates" for your dog with other animals you know to be healthy, and go someplace where strange dogs won't join in the play.

If you pet or play with other dogs while you are away from home, always disinfect your hands with hand sanitizer before interacting with your dog.

Do this regardless of how many hours have passed. No one knows for certain how long the infectious agents that cause kennel cough can live on surfaces.

Try not to board your dog at a kennel, or take the animal to be groomed at an off-site location, especially during the warm summer months when kennel cough is more prevalent. If at all possible, hire pet sitters and groomers to come to your home.

Kennel Cough in Rescue Shelters

Kennel cough can represent a moral dilemma in the rescue shelter environment. Many dogs are already infected with the condition when they are admitted to the facility.

If not, they will likely develop kennel cough immediately just from the stress of being in the shelter with strange humans, strange dogs, too much noise, too many lights, and not enough privacy. A dog's immune system is as sensitive as our own. With enough stressors, any animal will become sick.

In shelters with inadequate funds and staffing, kennel cough can be the basis for needless euthanasia. Deemed "too sick to adopt," thousands of animals die every day from a condition that can be completely cured with isolation and less than $100 / £65 in care.

Shelters actively seek volunteers who will take dogs out of the facility and foster them at home in quarantine until their symptoms resolve. The goal of any shelter is to limit the presence of kennel cough among their population while maintaining strict vaccination protocols and standards of cleanliness and sterilization. The hallmarks of controlling kennel cough in a rescue shelter include:

- vaccination
- isolation of infected animals
- thorough cleaning and sterilization
- adequate ventilation

(Be aware that if you are adopting a dog that will come into a home with existing pets, a quarantine of at least a week will be recommended, as well as kennel cough vaccinations for the animals already living in your home.)

Disease Control Measures

When an outbreak of kennel cough does occur in any facility where multiple dogs are routinely housed, ventilation should be increased to at least 12-20 complete air exchanges per hour.

Any new dogs entering the facility should be quarantined or otherwise isolated for their own protection for a period of 10-14 days.

All cages and equipment should be cleaned and disinfected daily, and employees should wash their hands and use hand sanitizer before and after handling any animal.

All bedding should be washing in hot water with both soap and bleach.

Afterword

The true impact of kennel cough in canines has nothing to do with the severity of the disease. Though highly contagious, this common respiratory condition generally resolves on its own in no more than 10 days with nothing more than palliative care.

(It is then advisable to follow up with an additional week to two weeks of isolation while the animal remains potentially contagious.)

The real tragedy is the role kennel cough plays in the annual euthanizing of 6-8 million shelter dogs deemed "too sick to adopt" because the facility cannot afford the approximately $100 / £65 in treatment required to allow the infection to pass.

Caused singularly or collectively by at least three viruses and six strains of bacteria, kennel cough does have the potential to morph into a more serious case of pneumonia in some cases.

Developing pneumonia becomes a concern when a secondary bacterial infection is present and when the patient is very young, very old, or immunosuppressed.

The infectious agents live in the warm, moist environment of the windpipe and upper airways, easily becoming airborne when a dog coughs. For this reason, any facility where groups of dogs are routinely present (shelters, day cares, dog shows, and the like) require vaccinations even though the preparation does not guarantee 100% protection.

All responsible pet owners should have a working understanding of kennel cough in order to recognize the condition early and seek appropriate veterinary intervention. This is especially crucial as many canine illnesses that are more serious my present with a cough.

For the most part, however, kennel cough is a manageable though often recurrent disease. A dog that has the condition once does not gain immunity against a second infection.

With vigilant observation and conservative care from its master, however, kennel cough is simply an unpleasant but survivable form of canine bronchitis.

Kennel Cough – Quick Facts Sheet

You may also see kennel cough referred to as:

- Canine Infectious Respiratory Disease Complex (CIRDC)
- Infectious tracheobronchitis
- Canine infectious respiratory disease

Infectious agents associated with the disease include, but are not limited to:

- canine parainfluenza virus
- canine adenovirus 2 (canine distemper virus)
- canine adenovirus 1
- bordetella bronchiseptica (the most common bacteria)
- streptococcus
- pasteurella
- pseudomonas
- e. coli
- mycoplasma

Contributing Factors:

- stress
- high rate of contact with other dogs

Susceptibility

All dogs, but in particular those that are:

55

- unvaccinated
- have a compromised immune system
- between the ages of 6 weeks and 6 months
- elderly

Helpful Steps in Prevention:

- reduction of crowding
- reduction of stress
- increased ventilation
- vigilant sanitation and sterilization
- isolating infected individuals

Vaccination

Kennel cough cannot be completely prevented by vaccination, but both the bordatella vaccine and that for canine distemper are useful in lowering the risk of infection.

Puppies should receive their first vaccinations at 4–6 weeks of age, with boosters every 2-3 weeks until age 16-18 weeks.

Treatment

In most cases dogs are treated symptomatically only, often with over-the-counter cough suppressants. Antibiotics are typically used only when a fever or severe coughing is present. If the disease progresses to pneumonia, other medications might be indicated.

Potential Complications

The most common complications of kennel cough are secondary bacterial infections and/or pneumonia.

Estimated Cost of Care in the Absence of Complications –
$100 / £65

Kennel Cough – Quick Facts Sheet

Relevant Websites

Adenovirus 1 in Dogs
www.petmd.com/dog/conditions/infectious-
parasitic/c_dg_canine_hepatitis#.Ue6MvmTOuXo

American Kennel Club Canine Health Foundation
www.akcchf.org/

American Heartworm Society
www.heartwormsociety.org/

Canine: Infectious Respiratory Disease Complex
www.sheltermedicine.com/node/31

Kennel Cough: An In-Depth Look
www.petmd.com/dog/general-
health/evr_dg_kennel_cough_an_indepth_look#.Ue6OO2T
OuXo

Petfinder: Kennel Cough by Dr. Lila Miller, D.V.M, ASPCA
http://www.petfinder.com/pro/for-shelters/kennel-cough/

UC Davis Koret Shelter Medicine program:
www.sheltermedicine.com

CIRDC information sheet:
sheltermedicine.com/portal/is_infectious_tracheobronchitis
_canine.shtml#top3

Canine Distemper information sheet:

sheltermedicine.com/portal/is_canine_distempervirus.shtm
l#top3

Canine Influenza information sheet:
sheltermedicine.com/portal/is_canine_influenza_update.sht
ml#top3

Frequently Asked Questions

What causes kennel cough?

A variety of agents may cause a case of kennel cough either individually or in combination. The possible culprits include viral and bacterial sources.

Viral Agents:

- canine parainfluenza virus
- canine adenovirus 2 (canine distemper virus)
- canine adenovirus 1

Bacterial Agents:

- bordetella bronchiseptica
- streptococcus
- pasteurella
- pseudomonas
- e. coli
- mycoplasma

Is my dog more at risk of catching kennel cough at a kennel or daycare?

No matter how well run a pet care facility may be, having your dog there will always increase the chances of the animal contracting kennel cough. Simply being in the presence of other dogs that may be contagious is a risk factor, but also in these settings your dog will be excited and potentially stressed. Under these conditions, the animal will be more vulnerable to infection.

The more frequently a dog visits a day care or kennel, however, the greater its chances of acquiring immunity against the disease. Typically only a small percentage of exposed dogs in a kennel cough outbreak actually become symptomatic.

Can kennels and daycares prevent kennel cough outbreaks?

No amount of preventive measures can completely guarantee that any facility can stop an outbreak of kennel cough. The cleanest facilities with the best ventilation and the most room that immediately quarantine infected animals can still experience major outbreaks because the disease is so contagious.

Really good kennels and day cares require that their clients be immunized against kennel cough, and they will not accept a dog that obviously has the illness. These facilities also follow strict sanitation practices and actively monitor for any sign of sickness in their client animals.

Are kennels and day care facilities the only place that kennel cough occurs?

The viruses that are the main causes of kennel cough can exist anywhere and, since they are airborne, can travel great distances. A dog that never leaves its backyard can come down with kennel cough.

Being in the presence of multiple dogs obviously raises the animal's risk. This kind of exposure can happen playing in the park, running loose around the neighborhood, visiting the vet, or in places like kennels, day cares, and dog shows.

My dog had the vaccine and developed kennel cough anyway. Why?

The standard vaccine used guards against infections caused by the Bordetella bacteria only. It does not offer immunity against cases of kennel cough caused by other bacteria or by viruses. While the vaccine does have its shortcomings, it has proven to be useful in decreasing the number and severity of infections in shelters, kennels, day cares, and at dog shows.

How is the kennel cough vaccine administered?

The vaccine may be administered by injection or as nose drops. Some vets favor nose drops in an effort to boost local immunity in the mucous membranes of the nose, throat and windpipe.

How can I tell if my dog has canine influenza or kennel cough?

The only way to make a definitive diagnosis is for swabs taken from the dog's nose and throat to be tested in a lab. If the dog's symptoms are mild, and the animal is alert and eating, such testing usually is not done.

If, however, the dog is lethargic, has a fever, and is not eating, your vet should recommend these tests as well as blood work and potentially chest x-rays to determine the true nature of the animal's illness.

Why are canine respiratory infections so contagious?

Because the viruses and bacteria that cause kennel cough live in the dog's airways, they are released every time the animal coughs. The action of the cough literally sprays the infection into the air.

Dogs with kennel cough should be kept isolated for at least a week until all their symptoms have resolved because they are still highly contagious.

Once my dog has been exposed to kennel cough, how long before the symptoms appear, and what will they be?

The incubation period will last from 2-14 days before a dry, hacking cough appears. The dog will sound as if it's trying to clear its throat, or even cough something up as in the "dry heaves." Also expect a thin, runny discharge from the nose.

In more serious cases, the animal will be lethargic, refuse to eat, and run a temperature. This is more typical in older dogs, or those with a suppressed immune system.

Most cases of kennel cough are mild, resolving in 1-2 weeks, but it is still important to have the animal examined by a veterinarian. In some rare cases, kennel cough can turn into a life-threatening case of pneumonia.

My vet prescribed oral antibiotics, but my dog's cough got worse. Why?

Even in dogs with a mild case of kennel cough, the coughing itself becomes a vicious cycle. It starts because of inflammation in the throat, and then the inflammation becomes worse due to the coughing!

As a guideline, watch to make sure your dog's coughing is not preventing the animal from eating, drinking, and sleeping. If this is the case, ask your vet to prescribe a cough suppressant.

Give the infection time to run its course. The coughing typically will last 1-2 weeks even when an antibiotic is administered. Stay in touch with your vet during this period, reporting on the dog's behavior.

It is extremely difficult for owners to listen to the coarse, rasping cough that dogs exhibit with this condition, especially since it can go on for 24 hours a day.

The important thing is to watch the dog's demeanor. As long as the animal is alert, remains active, and eats, you both just have to endure the cough until it begins to clear on its own.

Is there any homemade cough syrup I can give my dog?

Honey and lemon have been used for sore throats and coughs in both humans and animals for centuries. For your dog, try this recipe:

2 tbsp of honey
1 tsp of lemon juice
1/2 cup of water.

Administer twice daily roughly according to these measurements:

1 tbsp for a 50 lb dog
1/2 tbsp for a 25 lb dog
1/4 tbsp for a 12 lb dog
1/8 tbsp for a 6 lb dog

Glossary

A

acute disease - Any type of illness characterized by a sudden and rapid manifestation of symptoms.

acquired immunity – Immunity derived from an initial infection that provides acquired protection against re-infection.

adjunct therapy – Treatments that are secondary in nature and design to be supportive of a primary treatment.

adverse effect – Undesirable or unintentional side effects of a treatment protocol.

B

best practice – A phrase used in any branch of medicine to describe treatments that are broadly accepted as appropriate and that are in common use.

Blastomycocis – A fungal infection found in dogs that have come into contact with decaying wood and soil containing the infectious spores. Similar to a yeast infection. The condition is potentially fatal.

booster vaccination – Any vaccination administered at periodic intervals after a primary injection for the purpose of maintaining immunity to a disease.

Bordetella bronchiseptica - A bacterium related to the B. pertussis pathogen in humans that causes whooping cough. In dogs, the bordetella bronchiseptica is the leading bacterial cause of kennel cough or bronchitis.

C

canine distemper – A serious, highly contagious, and potentially fatal viral infection that presents with acute upper respiratory symptoms, fever, vomiting, diarrhea, pronounced depression, and various neurological deficits.

cardiomyopathy – A serious heart disease in dogs causing enlargement of the cardiac muscle and the accumulation of fluid. The exact cause of the condition is unknown.

carrier – A dog that carries a disease-causing agent in its system, but does not exhibit symptoms. Although immune itself, a carrier can pass the disease on to other animals.

chest – On a dog, the chest is that part of the trunk or body enclosed by or partially encircled by the rib cage.

chronic disease - A disease with an indefinite and potentially permanent presence in the system.

complementary and alternative medicine – Any type of medicine that is used in addition to a standard treatment is said to be complementary. Medicines used in place of generally accepted remedies are said to be alternative. Typically, complementary and alternative techniques have not undergone the same level of research and clinical testing as standard approaches. Such treatments may include, but are not limited to the use of dietary supplements including large doses of vitamins, herbal preparations including teas, acupuncture, acupressure, massage, magnet therapy, and various forms of spiritual healing.

D

disseminated disease – A disseminated disease is one that has spread entirely through an organ or through the entire body.

distemper – A highly contagious viral infection in dogs marked by depressed appetite, thick discharge from the eyes and nose, fever, lethargic behavior, and partial paralysis. The illness is potentially fatal.

E

euthanasia – The purposeful ending of a life in order to relieve suffering from an incurable illness. In companion animals this is usually accomplished with a lethal injection, most often an overdose of anesthetic that stops the heart.

F

fever – For dogs, a fever is said to be present if the reading is 103 F / 39.4 C or above.

fungus – Primitive forms of plant life that can be parasitic and infectious in nature. An example in companion animals would be ringworm.

G

gastric – Anything involving or related to the stomach.

H

heartworm – In dogs, the larval stage of the parasite Dirofilaria immitis enters the system via a mosquito bite. The adult worm lodges in the right side of the heart causing progressive symptoms that originate with a persistent and deep cough.

homeopathic – The treatment of a disease via a method calling for minute doses of a remedy to be given to a healthy animal to produce mild disease symptoms for the purposes of gradually cultivating immunity.

I

immunity – Protection against contracting a contagious disease developed wither by having been vaccinated against the condition or as a consequence of having survived a previous infection.

immunosuppressed – An individual who, for various reasons, has a lowered immune response and is thus more susceptible to disease. This is often the case in the aftermath of chemotherapy, for instance.

immune response – A complex series of defensive reactions triggered in the body in reaction to the presence of an infection.

immunization – Inoculations for the purpose of cultivating immunity against an infectious disease.

inflammation – A protective reaction initiated by tissues in response to infection, injury, or irritation. Common characteristics are redness, swelling, pain, and occasionally loss or diminishment of function.

injection – Liquid medication introduced into the body via a syringe.

intra-nasal – Medication introduced into the body as a nasal mist or drop.

M

mucous membranes – The epithelial tissues of the body that line the respiratory passages and secrete mucous.

P

parainfluenza – A flu-like infection in dogs that presents with fever, diarrhea, and vomiting.

pathogen – Any agent including microorganisms like bacterium or fungus that are responsible for causing disease.

pericarditis – A condition in which the membrane around the heart becomes inflamed.

V

vaccine – A serum created from dead or weakened pathogens including bacteria and viruses, or some part of these agents, for the purpose of stimulating antibody production when injected or otherwise introduced into the system. The end goal is the development of immunity against infection.

Valley Fever – This canine fungal infection occurs most often in low desert regions of the Southwest including Arizona, New Mexico, and parts of Texas. In its early stages, Valley Fever presents with a cough that can be mistaken for kennel cough.

virus – Simple submicroscopic bacteria, plants, or animals that often cause disease. A virus basically consists of a core RNA or DNA encased in a coat of protein. Without a host cell, a virus cannot replicate and therefore is not considered a living organism.

Z

zoonosis – Any disease present in animals that can be transmitted to humans. Common examples include rabies and psittacosis.

CPSIA information can be obtained at www.ICGtesting.com
Printed in the USA
LVOW12s2150031113

359856LV00016B/225/P

9 780989 658409